Mary Had a Baby

An Advent Bible Study
Based on African American Spirituals

CHERYL KIRK-DUGGAN
& MARILYN E. THORNTON

Abingdon Press
Nashville

MARY HAD A BABY

AN ADVENT BIBLE STUDY
BASED ON AFRICAN AMERICAN SPIRITUALS

Library of Congress Cataloging-in-Publication Data

ISBN: 978-1-426-79551-0

14 15 16 17 18 19 20 21 22 23 — 10 9 8 7 6 5 4 3 2 1

Manufactured in the United States of America

✳ Contents ✳

✳ Opening Meditation ✳

ADVENT

It is a time of expectation and anxiety.
It is a day when we tell the old, old story of Jesus and his love.

We remember how you came, Lord, and we anxiously await your return.
You promised to return, and like Israel in the days of old, we expectantly await the fulfillment of your promise.
It is hard down here, Lord, and we know that you know all about it.
They *treated you mean; treat us mean too!*
Your body [would be] broken, but you came anyway.
They made you be born in a manger, but you came anyway.
Our eyes was blind, but you came anyway.
We didn't know who you were.
And so, *sweet, little Jesus boy,* we gather today, looking for you to show up in our celebration [and in our study], as we wait for you to come again,
All grown up, with all power in your hands. Hallelujah!

✳ Introduction ✳

The birth of Jesus is celebrated in many kinds of songs: carols, hymns, oratorios and cantatas, and the African American spiritual. And yet the season of Advent is not just preparation for the Christmas season: putting up decorations, buying presents, baking treats, and lighting candles. The Advent season is the preparation in our hearts for the second coming of Jesus Christ. The season serves as our confession that even though we did not know who Jesus was when God came wrapped in flesh the first time, we are cultivating a value system that embraces the hope, joy, transformation, and communal healing that will be realized when Christ returns. African American spirituals provide an excellent medium by which to cross the divide between the first and second coming of Christ. Through them, all people can come to a better understanding of the unconditional love, justice, mercy, hope, faith, and community that Jesus brings for the flourishing of all God's children.

The African American spiritual represents a unique form in sacred music. The theology of spirituals speaks not only of God "who sits high and looks low" but one who profoundly and unequivocally identifies with those experiencing a world of cruelty, injustice, poverty, racism, and oppression. As the spiritual "Sweet Little Jesus Boy" describes, "They treat you mean, Lord; treat me mean, too! But that's the way it is down here." As a song form, the spiritual reflects the African origins, social context, musical vocabulary, Christian ethos, and biblical knowledge of the enslaved black people who created it. The songs in this Advent study point to the Messiah/Christ, about whom Isaiah prophesied: "Nations will come to your light and kings to your dawning radiance" (Isaiah 60:3). Yes, in the midst of opposites being drawn together, God's pulling down the powerful, lifting up the lowly, feeding the hungry, and sending the rich away empty (Luke 1:52-53) "a little child"— whom Christians believe to be sweet, little Jesus boy, Mary's baby—"will lead them" (Isaiah 11:6).

Mary Had a Baby: An Advent Bible Study Based on African American Spirituals utilizes four songs: "Mary Had a Baby," "Rise Up, Shepherd, and Follow," "Children, Go Where I Send Thee," and "Go, Tell It on the Mountain." The lessons will engage the birth narratives of Christ as found in the Gospels of Matthew and Luke and will invite us to a time of rebirth and renewal, to not only welcome the Christ Child but the coming Reign of God. Prepare your heart by listening to and singing along with the downloadable selections, by interpreting the lyrics, by searching the Scripture, and by committing to living out the gifts of the Nativity in the twenty-first century.

LESSON ONE

✳ Mary Had a Baby ✳

Mary had a baby, oh Lord!
Mary had a baby, oh my Lord!
Mary had a baby, oh Lord!
The people keep a-coming and the train done gone.

Verses

1. *What did she name him?*   2. *She named him Jesus.*
3. *Where was he born?*   4. *Born in a stable.*
5. *Where did she lay him?*   6. *She laid him in a manger.*

KEY VERSE: *Look! You will conceive and give birth to a son, and you will name him Jesus.* (LUKE 1:31)

LUKE 1:30-31

30 The angel said, "Don't be afraid, Mary. God is honoring you. 31 Look! You will conceive and give birth to a son, and you will name him Jesus."

MATTHEW 1:18-25

18 This is how the birth of Jesus Christ took place. When Mary his mother was engaged to Joseph, before they were married, she became pregnant with the Holy Spirit. 19 Joseph her husband was a righteous man. Because he didn't want to humiliate her, he decided to call off their engagement quietly. 20 As he was thinking about this, an angel from the Lord appeared to him in a dream and said, "Joseph son of David, don't be afraid to take Mary as your wife, because the child she carries was conceived by the Holy Spirit. 21 She will give birth to a son, and you will call him Jesus, because he will save his people from their sins." 22 Now all of this took place so that what the Lord had spoken through the prophet would be fulfilled:

23 *Look! A virgin will become pregnant and give birth to a son,*
And they will call him Emmanuel. (*Emmanuel* means "God with us.")

24 When Joseph woke up, he did just as an angel from God commanded and took Mary as his wife. 25 But he didn't have sexual relations with her until she gave birth to a son. Joseph called him Jesus.

Meditation

Babies are awe inspiring! The birth of any child is a miracle that in the best of circumstances begins with conception in a loving relationship. So much more the case with Mary's baby, conceived by the power of the Holy Spirit because of God's love for humanity. A scared, pregnant, and unmarried teen, Mary went off into the Judean highlands to visit her older cousin Elizabeth, who was also expecting. When Mary entered the home of Zechariah and Elizabeth, Elizabeth's baby jumped for joy (Luke 1:44) inside her womb. Mary then began to praise God for her situation. Rather than being scared, she celebrated a sacred trust; rather than being fearful, she accepted that she had been favored. She recognized God as being one who can turn any situation around, raising up those of low estate, and humbling the proud. Rather than feeling punished, she knew that her baby was one of promise. Mary had a baby, oh my Lord!

Prayer
Dear God,

Help us to know that every baby is your baby, one for whom we should anxiously await and gladly welcome. Help us to know that each child represents wonderful possibilities for new life in a brand new world. In Jesus' name. Amen.

Watching, Waiting, Wondering (Luke 1:30-31)

Most families know the watching, waiting, and wondering of expecting a baby. What is it going to be? Will the baby be a girl or boy? What shall we name him or her? How will we decorate the room? What clothes should we buy? Pregnancy is a time of waiting. Once the pregnancy has been determined, family members watch for signs of growth. The baby moved! It's kicking! May I touch your stomach? Ah, here is the head!

These days, there are sonograms and all the tests of modern technology for answers. Sometimes an ailment is diagnosed and surgery can be performed in the womb. Of course, Mary and Joseph had a much more secure sign than even the tools of twenty-first century technology. They had a message from God that the baby would be a boy so healthy he would save the people from their sins. And even as the angel told Mary, "Don't be afraid!" pregnancy, especially a first one, is always scary.

But then, Mary had the baby. Oh my Lord! There is wonderment and awe. People may know the mechanics of the birth process; but when new life emerges, we are still amazed. And while all births are miraculous, the magnitude and power of the gift of the Christ Child called forth a divine proclamation. God loves humanity so much that God sent a gift of the Christ

Child to come and show us how to live. How can we keep from singing? How could even those enslaved in America's "peculiar institution" not express the awe of that baby, who like them slept in a rough bed, layered with straw?

Each verse of "Mary Had a Baby" continues the story. Mary had a baby! What did she name him? She named him Jesus. Where was he born? Where did she lay him? In a stable, in a manger. Naming is important in the Bible as well as in African cultures, with naming rituals occurring on the eighth day after birth. The name indicates the new person's character and the expectations of the community. Both Mary and Joseph were told to name the baby, Jesus (Luke 1:31; Matthew 1:21). Jesus is the Greek version of the Hebrew name Yeshua or Joshua, meaning "YHWH (God) is salvation." Jesus would grow up to save, to deliver, and to liberate people from death-dealing circumstances.

Discussion Questions
1. How are children named in your family and community?
2. How do names affect the social reception of children as they mature?

This Train Is Bound for Glory

In this version of "Mary Had a Baby," every stanza ends with the refrain: "The people keep a-comin' and the train done gone." Along with the African American spiritual, trains were a new reality in the emerging industrial age of the early nineteenth century. Trains connected places that had been previously isolated, representing a way out, whether physical, spiritual, or imaginative. Train imagery figures prominently in African American lore. In the spiritual "Get on Board, Little Children," "The gospel train is coming. I hear the car wheels movin' and rumblin' through the land." People are challenged to reach the land of spiritual freedom.

There is also the historical image of the Underground Railroad, with conductors who led passengers (escapees) to stations (safe houses) on the way to physical freedom in the North. As the century progressed, there were the real trains that ran through tunnels built by heroes of legend such as John Henry, who died in a contest with a steam drill (invented in 1870). Even in the midst of the Civil Rights Movement (1960s), the Impressions were singing about trains. "People get ready, there's a train a-comin.' Don't need no ticket; you just thank the Lord!" In every case, the train is bound for a more glorious state of being, moving toward liberation and opportunity.

What did the slaves mean by placing the image of Mary's newborn baby beside that of a train station? "The people keep a-comin' and the train done gone." The phrase may constitute a spiritual warning. Mary's baby represents freedom, salvation, and deliverance, "Oh my Lord!" Do not miss your opportunity to worship him. Jesus is the way out from sin and death. Don't be too late! This phrase, however, could also constitute a reality check. On many plantations, Christmas was the one time of year in which everyone was allowed to relax, making it a better time to attempt an escape from slavery. In *Roots: The Gift* (often shown on TV during the Christmas season), Alex Haley reconstructs how an escape at Christmas might have been accomplished more easily. While the slaveholders and their guests at the big house were partying, the slaves in the quarters might plan a get-away. The television version demonstrates how utterly important it was for potential runaways to get to the meeting place on time. Don't be too late! You don't want the train/the conductor to be gone by the time you get there.

In "Mary Had a Baby," awe and wonder are side by side with reality. Eschatology, the branch of theology that is concerned with the end times, of which Advent is a part, is mediated by the narrative of what must be done right now. You've got to take care of that baby. With feet firmly grounded in their present situation, proclaiming a way out of oppression, in one simple song these enslaved theologians retold the story of Jesus' birth and expressed the end-time belief and the present reality that some might get left behind. You might get left behind in slavery if you are not ready to go. You may also miss the opportunity to experience eternal freedom if you do not take care of the business at hand.

Another spiritual expresses it a different way: "I got shoes, you got shoes, all God's children got shoes. When I get to heaven, gonna put on my shoes and gonna walk all over God's heaven. Everybody talkin' 'bout heaven ain't going there, heaven!" This speaks to a readiness for the coming of God's justice. As a child born in poverty, Mary's baby would not have shoes any more than the slaves did. Like Mary's baby, they were presently lying on a bed of straw; but they planned to be on that train to a brighter tomorrow. By faith they awaited a train that was bound for glory, where they could walk all over God's heaven and be free in that life from those who would deny them freedom in this one.

Discussion Questions

1. *How does this spiritual enlarge your understanding of African American history and culture?*
2. *How do the biblical story and the story of American slavery complement and/ or challenge each other?*

Immanuel (Matthew 1:18-25)

Matthew sets the stage with an account of Jesus' genealogy (1:1-17). He wants to prove to his audience that the story is about a Hebrew and a figure of royal lineage. The story is about Jesse's family. His son David brought the tribes of Israel, the Hebrew children, to unity and glory. Particular women such as David's grandmother Ruth are also included. The account also serves to remind of God's saving action in history. From the nomad Abraham to King David, from exile in Babylon to the return to Judea, God was present. God was with the people. After this appropriate introduction, Matthew is now ready to tell the story. Here's what happened:

Mary and Joseph were engaged. In ancient times, *betrothal* meant that couples were as good as married legally and socially but not sexually. Joseph had a dilemma. He had observed the social mores of the day and refrained from sexual relations with Mary during their engagement, but Mary came up pregnant. By law, Joseph could have had Mary stoned to death. Her pregnancy appeared to be evidence of her unfaithfulness to him and to the community. The penalty for adultery was death (Deuteronomy 22:13-21). Because Joseph was a righteous man, he did not want to expose her to public humiliation and death. After making the decision to call off the engagement quietly, Joseph received a revelation from an angel. In a dream, the angel told Joseph that Mary had conceived by the power of the Holy Spirit and not to be afraid. The angel also provided the child's name: Jesus. In verse 23, the angel makes the link with Old Testament prophecy, telling Joseph that Mary's baby is part of the promise of salvation for God's people, an indication that God has not forgotten; God is with us still. A young woman has conceived and will bear a baby boy. He will be called Immanuel, "God is with us." Joseph awoke and obeyed the voice of God by completing the contract with Mary, marrying her and naming the baby Jesus.

By singing about the birth of a Savior so long ago, by acknowledging the arrival of Immanuel, the enslaved demonstrated an understanding that even in slavery God was present as they brought forth new generations. Hope is the gift every child brings to the world. Each child carries the light of God within by which it may receive the gospel of Jesus Christ. Every pregnant woman bears a potential liberator, one who may be anointed to increase freedom and justice in the world and point someone to Jesus Christ. The gift of new life and the presence of Immanuel help us experience the immediacy of God right here and right now.

Discussion Questions

1. *What can we learn about family dynamics from the interactions of angels, God, Mary, and Joseph?*
2. *How have you experienced God's presence during Advent? How do you experience it during the Christmas season?*

Twenty-first Century Nativity: Honoring Mother and Child

Too many in twenty-first century America take for granted that a pregnant woman will have a safe delivery. Yet throughout the world, childbirth remains a major cause of death for mother and child. In fact, the African American infant mortality rate of 13.1 per 1,000 is higher than that of Romania (11 per 1,000), and more than double the rate of white American women (5.6 per 1,000), which is beaten by Japan (2.6) and many other countries, although not by any in Africa or South America.* Studies show that while lifestyle choices (smoking, obesity, HIV/AIDS) can make an impact, the mortality rate is the same for black women without these factors. Birth weight is also important. A 2007 study in Chicago revealed that the birth weight of babies born to first-generation African and Caribbean women dropped to 6.8 pounds compared with their immigrant mothers' babies (7.3 pounds), while the babies of white women remained at 7.5 pounds. Befuddled doctors concluded that the stress of racism, endured by black women spending their entire lives in America, affects mother and child.**

For children born during slavery, their families knew that they were being born into hard times. In slavery, it could mean the disruption of a family line by means of the auction block. Nevertheless, in hope the ancestors would always ask a question at the birth of each child, "Is this the one?" "Is this [our Moses], the one who will get us out of slavery?" "Is this the one through whom God will bring salvation?" In childbirth, mother and child are performing a sacred act. What would happen if we were to greet every birth as an indication of the promise of God's love and saving purpose in the world?

While neither Mary nor Joseph speak in Matthew's birth narrative, our featured song returns Mary's voice to her. Mary is questioned. Mary names. Mary acts. Perhaps the powerless slaves identified with the many women of the Bible whose voices and names are often obscured. In the twenty-first century, the people of God are called to acknowledge and listen to the voices of mothers, women, and girls. Girls and boys must be taught self-respect and the importance of speaking for themselves: not letting others rob them of their voices or put words in their mouths. Let us remember the case of 2013 Nobel Peace Prize nominee Malala Yousafzai, a Pakistani schoolgirl (born in 1997) who in 2012 was shot in the head in a botched assassination attempt, for speaking in favor of education for women. In the twenty-first century, we must advocate equality for women in every aspect of life, including the church. Honoring mothers is a first step in honoring all people.

The next step is to honor the children. It is hypocritical to drool over the Christ Child while failing to be concerned about the birth, health, and wealth of children in the twenty-first century. For more than 30 years, Marian

Wright Edelman has honored children through the nonprofit advocacy organization she founded in 1973. Through the Children's Defense Fund, Edelman is striving to level the playing field for children through education, health insurance, food programs, housing, and violence prevention.***

While Mary's story is one of the divine hand at work in human history, it can be interpreted as a cautionary tale on teen pregnancy. Her potential plight is a reminder that parenting is not a game and bringing children into the world and raising them is a shared responsibility. Having sex outside the covenant of marriage can lead to a serious situation. What happens if Joseph is not honorable? Critical to loving the Lord, our neighbor, and ourselves is cherishing the sacredness of our bodies, respecting the bodies of others (thus doing no harm), and honoring the gift of sexuality and procreation. As such, our beliefs are foundational to our values and our activity. And yet children are not responsible for how they come into this world. The children keep a-comin'. We must be the train in the station that welcomes the gift of life, and honors mother and child, living with hope for the salvation of our community through Jesus Christ our Lord.

Discussion Questions

1. *The number of children born out of wedlock in the black community has actually decreased in the twenty-first century. What do you think accounts for this?*
2. *What can churches do to help children in their communities flourish?*

References

*http://open.salon.com/blog/howard_steven_friedman/2012/06/26/us_infant_mortality_rate_higher_than_other_wealthy_countries

**http://rolandmartinreports.com/blog/2012/11/washington-watch-why-are-infant-mortality-rates-so-high-among-african-americans-video/

***http://www.childrensdefense.org/about-us/

LESSON TWO

✳ Rise Up, Shepherd, and Follow ✳

Verse 1
There's a star in the east on Christmas morn; rise up, shepherd, and follow. It will lead to the place where the Christ was born; rise up, shepherd, and follow.

Verse 2
If you take good heed to the angel's words; rise up, shepherd, and follow. You'll forget your flocks, you'll forget your herds; rise up, shepherd, and follow.

Refrain
Follow, follow, rise up, shepherd, and follow; ~~rise up, shepherd, and follow.~~ *last time*
Follow the star of Bethlehem; rise up, shepherd, and follow.

KEY VERSE: *When they heard the king, they went; and look, the star they had seen in the east went ahead of them until it stood over the place where the child was.* (MATTHEW 2:9)

LUKE 2:15

15 When the angels returned to heaven, the shepherds said to each other, "Let's go right now to Bethlehem and see what's happened. Let's confirm what the Lord has revealed to us."

MATTHEW 2:1-12

1 After Jesus was born in Bethlehem in the territory of Judea during the rule of King Herod, magi came from the east to Jerusalem. 2 They asked, "Where is the newborn king of the Jews? We've seen his star in the east, and we've come to honor him." 3 When King Herod heard this, he was troubled, and everyone in Jerusalem was troubled with him. 4 He gathered all the chief priests and the legal experts and asked them where the Christ was to be born. 5 They said, "In Bethlehem of Judea, for this is what the prophet wrote:

6 *You, Bethlehem, land of Judah, by no means are you least among the rulers of Judah, because from you will come one who governs, who will shepherd my people Israel.*

7 Then Herod secretly called for the magi and found out from them when the star had first appeared. 8 He sent them to Bethlehem, saying, "Go search carefully for the child. When you've found him, report to me so that I too may go

and honor him." 9 When they heard the king, they went; and look, the star they had seen in the east went ahead of them until it stood over the place where the child was. 10 When they saw the star, they were filled with joy. 11 They entered the house and saw the child with Mary his mother. Falling to their knees, they honored him. Then they opened their treasure chests and presented him with gifts of gold, frankincense, and myrrh. 12 Because they were warned in a dream not to return to Herod, they went back to their own country by another route.

Meditation

From Abel, a keeper of sheep (Genesis 4:2); to God, the shepherd of Psalm 23; to the reprobate shepherds of Israel (Ezekiel 34); to Jesus, the good shepherd (John 10:11), the image of shepherd is prominent in biblical literature. After his resurrection, Jesus instructed Peter to be a good shepherd, feed and take care of the sheep. However, it was only by following Jesus—that is, by being a sheep—that he could be the right kind of shepherd. "Follow me," said Jesus (John 21:15-19). When Jesus comes back, he will come as a shepherd-king, separating those who have followed his way, being sheep, from those who have not, being goats. His way is described as feeding the hungry, giving water to the thirsty, visiting the imprisoned, and caring for the sick (Matthew 25:31-46). As we await his return, let us rise up like the shepherds in the Judean highlands and lead others to and in the light of Jesus Christ.

Prayer
Dear God,
   Lead me and guide me with the bright light of your teachings. Give me the wisdom of the three kings and the faith of the shepherds, and let me rise from my complacency and follow you on the path to eternal life. In Jesus' name, amen.

Watching, Waiting, Wondering (Luke 2:15)

Anyone who is taking care of someone or something experiences an element of just watching, waiting, and wondering. New parents watch the new baby while she sleeps; they wait for her to cry, and then wonder why she is crying. Shepherds who watch over animals do quite a bit of waiting, especially at night. The words to one Christmas hymn state: "While shepherds watched their flocks by night, all seated on the ground. . . ." Can you imagine their surprise when "The angel of the Lord came down with glory all around, with glory all around"? This was out of the ordinary. You can imagine their wonderment. They decided to get up off of the ground and go to Bethlehem to follow up on the message of the angels.

But the shepherds were not the only ones who were watching, waiting, and wondering. There were astrologers in the East, the scientists of their day, wise men who studied the skies and the formation of the stars. Matthew reports that this priestly class discovered a new star either to the east or west of where they were situated. Both Persia (east) and Egypt (west) had a priestly class of wise men in their social system. If the star was in the east, it would mean that the travelers came from the west—Egypt or Ethiopia. Our spiritual, however, directs shepherds, rather than kings or wise men, to follow the star.

It was against the law for enslaved persons to read. They could only hear the stories concerning Jesus' birth. One such story was about wise men, and another was about shepherds. A conventional reading of Luke and Matthew make it difficult for some to harmonize a setting of royalty, wealth, and knowledgeable strangers with that of mangers and sheep. However, in a world in which African royalty, priests, and elders had become part of a chattel slavery system, in a world in which the creative imagination of the slave was not limited by convention or literacy, the two stories are reconciled in the spiritual "Rise Up, Shepherd, and Follow" with shepherds following the star.

Discussion Questions

1. *What are you watching and waiting for?*
2. *What events in the world are giving you either a sense of wonderment or a time of puzzled wondering?*

Arise, Shine, for Your Light Has Come

The role of shepherd certainly was relatable to the African American slave. Although very necessary to a functioning economy, in most cultures, shepherding is a dirty, isolating job, not unlike being a slave. Christmas, however, was a special time for those enslaved. The season was not only a time to celebrate the birth of Jesus, sometimes receiving small gifts or new clothing, it was a time to celebrate themselves. By replacing Matthew's priestly travelers with persons of lowly estate, the slave songsters subtly created a revolution in status for themselves. They became the wise seekers because they were following the star that leads to the place where salvation is found.

Nevertheless, many plantation owners were hesitant for slaves to become Christians. They thought that if slaves experienced spiritual liberation, they would also want physical liberation. From colonial times, laws were put in place to make sure that both the enslaved and the slaveholder understood that this was not to be. In 1664, Maryland was the first colony to pass a law stating that baptism had no effect on the social status of slaves. This put an end to judicial decisions that had freed slaves after baptism. North Carolina,

New Jersey, New York, South Carolina, and Virginia quickly followed this example. By 1671, the Maryland law was expanded to include Blacks who had been converted before enslavement. Slaveholders feared losing their investment. The lyrics for "Rise Up, Shepherd, and Follow," would have been ample proof for their concern.

In singing this song, the slaves admonished one another over and over to rise up and to follow. The words *rise up* and *follow* are repeated many times in a melody that rises with the words. The moderate, walking speed of this song helps emphasize the words, while the simple rhythmic structure enables the community to concentrate on word meanings. The community is encouraged to rise up, follow, listen (take good heed), and leave. If the master had really been listening, this song would have been banned just as the drum had been banned. Even the tempo of this spiritual implies the action and movement that is being celebrated by the slave community. It is a good walking song; it is a good rallying song. Black people were ingenious at putting messages into music. And despite the myth that enslaved Africans were harmless and happy, slaveholders from New England to the southern regions (especially Virginia) were all too aware that they had made plans to "rise up" since the 1660s. Through music, enslaved Blacks were able to communicate their determination to be freedom bound.

The song also reminds the community of faith to follow Jesus, that by getting to the place where Jesus is, they will find deliverance and salvation. They are admonished to leave everything else and seek first the kingdom of God (Matthew 6:33). During his ministry, Jesus told his disciples that they might have to leave home, family, traditions, and land in order to follow him (Luke 9:57-62). The African American slave knew what it meant to leave home, family, traditions, and land. Even those whose knowledge of Africa had disappeared from recent family memory had an awareness of being in a different place from where they were supposed to be.

Discussion Questions
1. Did this section give you any new information about American history?
2. What slave insurrections do you know about?

Searching and Seeking (Matthew 2:1-12)

In Hebrews 11, Abraham is commended for having the faith to leave his homeland to search for and seek a place he had never been before. Christian faith is all about searching and seeking, leaving that which is familiar to move onto a higher plane. "Rise Up, Shepherd, and Follow" admonishes its singers: "Leave your sheep, leave your rams, leave your ewes, leave your lambs. Follow!" As in so many spirituals, there is another layer of meaning. The song is not only about the birth of the Bright and Morning Star, Jesus Christ. For many, the star in the east represented Polaris, the North Star.

Frederick Douglass named his abolitionist newspaper *The North Star* as part of his campaign to advocate for the liberation of black people. Polaris is found by tracing in the sky the outline of constellations, the Big Dipper and the Little Dipper. The bottom of the cup in the Big Dipper leads to the handle of the Little Dipper, where Polaris shines forth. For those slaves desiring to seek Freedom Land, these star formations, probably better known as drinking gourds to the common person, might be the only help a runaway slave could expect to receive. In their creativity, those who were enslaved sewed quilts and made up songs indicating the way to go. One such song is "Follow the Drinking Gourd."

> *When the sun comes back and the first quail calls,*
> *Follow the Drinking Gourd.*
> *For the old man is waiting for to carry you to freedom,*
> *If you follow the Drinking Gourd.*

First published in 1928 by Lee Hays, "Follow the Drinking Gourd" gave freedom-seeking slaves instructions for connecting with the Underground Railroad. Because of its publication date, some historians posit that black slaves should not be credited for this song. Yet "Follow the Drinking Gourd" actually makes no sense, except for having originated in the historical context of the American slave system. From folk stories to jazz to rhythm and blues to hip-hop, black Americans are often divested of the fruits of their cultural genius while others receive credit and royalties. The song details that the best time to travel was after the winter solstice "when the sun comes back," when the sun's altitude is higher at noon. Quails migrated and spent the winters in the South. So those planning an escape learned to leave the plantation in the winter and travel by way of the drinking gourd. Ultimately, they would meet up with someone, perhaps an old man, who was an Underground Railroad conductor. This person would help them hide and/or would provide a boat or wagon for the rest of the journey. Or if no boat was available, escaping slaves could walk across the Ohio River when it was frozen. Like the wise men, who followed the stars in their search for a new king, the slaves followed the drinking gourd, seeking freedom.

Matthew, unlike some historians, was diligent in presenting an appropriate historical, political, and geographical setting. As the authority in charge of the province of Judea in the Roman Empire, Herod had the job of being aware of important events and activities in his jurisdiction. When the wise men/astrologers noticed the new star in the sky in the direction of Palestine, they interpreted it as a sign that something important was happening there. In both Egypt and Persia (Iran) were communities of Jews where Gentiles could have become familiar with the Hebrew writings and prophecies. Like curious intellectuals, they sought more knowledge by going to the source.

Jerusalem was the capital of ancient Israel and Judah, and it remained the center of Jewish life. What a logical place for the wise men to go! But their inquiry about a new king for Jews alarmed Herod. *He* was king. A new king meant trouble for him. So he ordered the priests and scribes to do research. By searching the Scriptures, they discovered that the Messiah (Christ) would be born in Bethlehem of Judea, right in Herod's jurisdiction. Leaving the religious experts out of it, Herod conferred with the wise men. He wanted to know: When did the star appear? The answer would give the approximate the age of the child. He sent them off, asking for a progress report upon their return so that he too could pay homage to the new king. As the wise men continued their journey, the star guided them to the exact spot where Jesus was. When they got to their destination, they were overjoyed. These wise men did not come empty-handed. They had made a long trip in order to pay homage to a king. The Ruler of the Universe had given this new child a star. In their joy, they gave the baby various treasures that would aid him in his life on earth. The wise men continued to follow the lead of God and took an alternative route home that bypassed the ill-intentioned Herod.

Discussion Questions

1. *What would happen in our society if we were to look at each child who is born as having a star, a special place in the universe?*
2. *How would we treat each one?*

Twenty-first Century Nativity: Following the Light

The spiritual "Rise Up, Shepherd, and Follow" admonishes the shepherds to rise up and follow the star of Bethlehem. In Luke, we see that shepherds did indeed leave their sheep to find out what the angels who lit up the sky were talking about. In Matthew, we find that the wise men left their homes, following a star that led them to the King of kings and Lord of lords. What are we willing to leave, to do differently; what route are we willing to take in order to anticipate a brighter future for all of God's children? Advent is about waiting and watching, but waiting on the Lord is not a twiddling-your-thumbs kind of prospect; it is a proactive, get-up-and-go activity.

If we follow the story, we find that after paying homage to Jesus, the wise men got up and went in a different direction in order to save the life of the child. Joseph and Mary did the same thing. Listening to the direction of God, they kept moving, not remaining in Bethlehem. But fortified with the gifts of the magi, they made their way to Egypt and stayed there until Herod died (Matthew 2:12-15). This happened because it had been Herod's intention all along to kill that baby. And he did not care how many children he had to kill in order to get to the Anointed One, the Messiah, the one who could and would save the people (Matthew 2:16).

What are we waiting for? Is not there evidence enough that black children and indeed all children are under attack? Just look at the numbers who do not graduate from high school: those who are killed on the street even in schools; those who take their lives through drug use, alcoholism, and suicide; and those who land in prison! Indeed, there is a prison-industrial complex that has been designed to receive them when they fail in the world. And what about the challenge of "Stand Your Ground" laws? The light of Jesus leads to freedom, to abundant life and love—that is—shalom, wholeness, not to social, emotional, mental, or spiritual death. It is time to do something different. Herod did not have the best interest of the Christ Child at heart. Who is it that has the best interest of today's children at heart?

This Advent season, contemplate on how the community of God can rise up and do something that will lead to freedom, where all of God's children will bask in the light of God. By being prayerful and open, we can have the energy to go on a journey that will create change in the world. By giving room for the power of the Holy Spirit in our lives, we can begin to experience some of the depths of God's glory and the ability of the Spirit to use us as change agents who work for a transformed world. Let us follow the light of Jesus Christ to a place where the first will be last and the last will be first (Matthew 19:27-30), where the glory of the Lord will be revealed and all flesh will see it together (Isaiah 40:5).

Discussion Questions

1. What is the effect on the black community of so many of its young men dying violently or going to prison?
2. What can churches do to equip parents to be the guiding light in the lives of their children?

Reference

The Chronological History of the Negro in America, by Peter M. Bergman and Mort N. Bergman (Mentor, 1969); pages 16–17.

LESSON THREE
✳ Children, Go Where I Send Thee ✳

Children, go where I send thee.
How shall I send thee?
I'm gonna send thee one by one.
One for the little, bitty baby
who's born, born, born in Bethlehem.
I'm gonna send you two by two.
Two for Joseph and Mary.
Three for the good, old wise men.
Four for the shepherds who knocked at the door.
Five for the animals in the stall.
Six for the stars that shone so bright.

Traditional version includes
Two for Paul and Silas.
Three for the Hebrew children.
Four for the four that stood at the door.
Five for the gospel preachers.
Six for the six that never got fixed.
Seven for the seven that never got to heaven.
Eight for the eight that stood at the gate.
Nine for the nine all dressed so fine.
Ten for the ten commandments.
Eleven for the eleven deriders.
Twelve for the twelve apostles.

KEY VERSE: *Since Joseph belonged to David's house and family line, he went up from the city of Nazareth in Galilee to David's city, called Bethlehem, in Judea.* (LUKE 2:4)

LUKE 2:1-7

1 In those days Caesar Augustus declared that everyone throughout the empire should be enrolled in the tax lists. 2 This first enrollment occurred when Quirinius governed Syria. 3 Everyone went to their own cities to be taxed. 4 Since Joseph belonged to David's house and family line, he went up from the city of Nazareth in Galilee to David's city, called Bethlehem, in Judea. 5 He

went to be enrolled together with Mary, who was promised to him in marriage and who was pregnant. **6** While they were there, the time came for Mary to have her baby. **7** She gave birth to her firstborn child, a son, wrapped him snugly, and laid him in a manger, because there was no place for them in the guest room.

Meditation

Before Mary had a baby and before the shepherds and wise men followed the light, Joseph took a journey with his very pregnant wife. He had to leave where he was in order to obey a governmental edict to be registered and taxed in his family home-place. Can you imagine? It is as if the descendants of those African Americans who left the rural South during the Great Migration, seeking industrial work in cities like Chicago and Detroit, had to return to the cotton fields of the Mississippi Delta to register to vote. Or those in New York City had to return to the orange groves of Florida to pay their taxes. Or those who went to California had to go back to the bayous of Louisiana in order to be counted in the census. It does not make much sense. But Joseph went where he was sent, to "The House of Bread," and there "The Bread of Life" was born, born, born in Bethlehem.

Prayer

Lord, sometimes it just doesn't make sense, the things we are required to do. But we trust the same omniscient God whom Joseph trusted. In this journey called Life, help us trust you even more. In Jesus' name, amen.

Watching, Waiting, Wondering

What imaginations the slaves had as they birthed "Children, Go Where I Send Thee"! Much has been made of European immigrants who figured out how to flee indentured peasantry and participate in the carving out of new countries in the Americas. They imagined freedom on land not owned and inherited by nobility, and they roamed that land until they found a portion on which to build their own heritage.

How unfortunate that the land they "found" belonged to another people, Native Americans! How unfortunate that some instituted an even more oppressive system than that from which they had escaped and imposed it on Africans whom they imported to America in chains! And yet that did not stop the Africans or their descendants from using their own imaginations to sing about the freedom of movement, going from one place to another. It did not stop them from watching, waiting, and wondering about a time when they, too, would be at liberty to go where God would send them.

The country wherein the enslaved imagined the freedom to determine their own destiny was from its very founding governed by laws that restricted their movement. The well-known Fugitive Slave Act of 1850* was only the second, harsher law that made it more difficult for persons deemed property, to go and stay free. The first Fugitive Slave Act was signed into law in 1793 as part of the U.S. Constitution by then-president George Washington. It authorized local governments to operate across state lines in order to seize and return escaped slaves to those claiming to own them, and it imposed penalties on anyone who helped in their escape. This unjust law could only have produced abuses as happened in the kidnapping of New York free Black Solomon Northrup** (also Northup), who was sold south to Louisiana and remained in slavery for twelve years. Freedom-loving people resisted these laws, creating secret networks such as the Underground Railroad, which provided assistance to freedom-seeking slaves. Some captured Blacks, like Shadrach Minkins in 1851, were even rescued from federal authority by Boston abolitionists.

During this critical time, the Negro spiritual came into being, tangible evidence of the hope of the slave. In the midst of oppression, suppression, and repression, Africans in America continued to watch, wait and hope for freedom by creating songs that expressed the ability "to go." In a land that continues to restrict the movement of people of color with varieties of "Stop and Frisk" and "Stand Your Ground" laws, let us not give up watching, waiting, and working for the coming of God's justice in our own world and when Jesus shall come again.

Discussion Questions

1. Are there similarities between the Fugitive Slave Acts and our immigration laws?
2. Did you see the movie 12 Years a Slave? Why, or why not?

A Theology of Movement

The folklore and ways of enslaved Africans indicate a knowledge and understanding of God that was somewhat oppositional to that of their masters. Some folk stories tell of individuals who escaped to freedom by supernatural means. In "The People Could Fly," slaves responded to wisdom words from an elder and escaped the cruelty of an overseer by sprouting wings and walking on the air to freedom. Some versions say that they turned themselves into buzzards. Another story is based on a slave revolt of Ibo tribesmen, who, in 1803, were transported to St. Simon's Island, South Carolina. Rather than submit to slavery, they ran aground their mutinied vessel at Dunbar's Creek and chose to walk back to Africa through the water. Some versions tell that as they walked, they sang and that the slaves looking on remembered the melody, later creating words that described what they had experienced.

O Freedom, O Freedom! O Freedom over me!
And before I'll be a slave, I'll be buried in my grave
And go home to my Lord and be free!

They had no illusions as to what happened to those resisting Ibos. With "Children, Go Where I Send Thee," the singers are transported in their minds to a state in which their bodies are free to live and move and have their being in God (Acts 17:28). All of this expresses a theology of movement, a search for wisdom or knowledge, thinking patterns, beliefs, concepts, and attitudes that connect all of these categories with what one believes about God. Their song reveals a belief in a God "who sits high and looks low," the only One to whom all of their entire movement and obedience is due.

I'm gonna sing when the Spirit says sing (3X)
And obey the Spirit of the Lord.

I'm gonna shout when the Spirit says shout (3X)
And obey the Spirit of the Lord.

Although slave owners believed that slaves were merely ignorant heathens, slaves were indeed creative, thinking individuals—whole persons, made in the image of God. Even as life in slavery severely restricted them in movement from place to place, in who could assemble, where and how many, through song slaves could experience the freedom to move in their spirits.

By singing "Children, Go" they were freed to follow the commandment of Jesus Christ, "Go, therefore and make disciples of all nations, baptizing them in the name of the Father and of the Son and of the Holy Spirit, and teaching them to obey everything I have commanded you" (Matthew 28:19-20). In their religious imaginations, they were freed to move to and be in all the places the biblical heroes and apostles mentioned in the song. In a world that sought to control even their religious meetings and right to assembly, they gathered one by one or ten by ten. They subversively taught and practiced counting as they sang about being sent out in varying numbers. They moved and clapped, and experienced joy and fulfillment in a pattern of movement that transported them away from the bonds of slavery into the freedom of salvation in Jesus Christ.

Discussion Question

How does imagination serve people who must operate in extremely difficult circumstances?

So, Where Would They Go? (Luke 2:1-7)

The first place the enslaved Africans' imaginations would take them is Rome, for that is from whence Caesar Augustus's burdensome edict came, that all people living in the Roman Empire should go to his hometown to be counted in a census and taxed. Rome was the seat of imperial power, a place of laws, where statutes were imposed so that the conquered could be further oppressed.

During the days of slavery, laws that allowed for the enslavement of human beings flowed from the capital city of the nation, Washington, D.C. There, the case of Dred Scott landed before the nation's highest court. Scott was a slave in Missouri who sued for his freedom in Missouri, citing the fact that he and his wife and children had been transported to Illinois and the Wisconsin Territory, where slavery was illegal. In 1857, in Dred Scott vs. Sanford, also known as the Dred Scott Decision, the Supreme Court ruled that Blacks were not citizens and had no rights, whether residing in states that practiced slavery or not. Yes, as the enslaved celebrated the birth of a Savior who came to release the prisoners and liberate the oppressed, their singing would transport them to Rome and other seats of power.

Luke also notes that Quirinius was the governor of Syria at the time the census was taken and that the land of Palestine was part of his territory. With this information, Luke provides the early church with a frame of reference concerning a historical time.

Next the slaves' melodious journey would have transported them to Nazareth in Galilee, where Joseph and Mary were living when the executive order was pronounced. Modern-day Nazareth, located in the North District of Israel, is considered "the Arab capitol of Israel," with a majority population of Israeli Arabs, who are 67 percent Muslim and 33 percent Christian. In Isaiah 9:1-2, Galilee is described as a land on the farthest most boundaries of Israel, beyond the Jordan, a non-Jewish "land of the Gentiles" (NRSV). Upon having an opportunity to meet Jesus, future disciple Nathanael asked, "Can anything from Nazareth be good?" (John 1:46). In the structured caste system of slavery, those singing, "Children, Go" would have been aware that similar judgments were being made of them. Can anything good come out of the cotton patch and the tobacco, sugar cane, and rice fields?

Can anything good come out of slave quarters? Slave quarters on large plantations such as George Washington's Mount Vernon in Virginia, were usually some distance away (farthest most boundaries) from the "big house," the master's mansion. In 1797, European visitors to Mount Vernon described the slave homes as "wretched," being poorly built with dangerous fireplaces and no place for beds. "We entered one of the huts of the Blacks, for one can not call them by the name of houses. They are more miserable than the most miserable cottages of peasants."*** The next stop in the Christmas narrative was to a similarly wretched place, animal quarters in Bethlehem because there was no room in the inn.

Joseph's ancestral line was from David, whose hometown was Bethlehem in Judea, some distance south of where he lived in Nazareth. But this was where he had to go and take the pregnant Mary, who was legally his wife, in order to meet the tax registration deadline. She, too, had to be enrolled. Who knows whether they got to register before the baby came. Luke tells us that when Jesus was born, Mary wrapped his body tightly in strips of cloth as was the custom. Then she laid him in a manger, which is a trough from which animals eat.

The French Christmas carol "The Friendly Beasts" imaginatively describes how each animal in the barn gave Jesus a gift. The donkey had carried Jesus' mother, the doves cooed him to sleep, the sheep gave wool to keep him warm, and the cow gave him the manger. They did this because Jesus was their brother "kind and good." Even in a lowly manger, Jesus was fulfilling prophecy.

> The wolf will live with the lamb,
> And the leopard will lie down with the young goat;
> The calf and the young lion will feed together,
> And a little child will lead them. (Isaiah 11:6)

Discussion Questions

1. *Once Joseph and Mary left Nazareth, they unwittingly became wandering refugees, unable to return home, though not permanently homeless. How can this understanding affect our attitude toward those who are homeless and/or displaced in our society and the world?*
2. *How do tax laws affect the well-being of people?*

Twenty-first Century Nativity: Going Where the Children Are

As we celebrate Advent and the creative imagination of those who produced the spiritual "Children, Go Where I Send Thee," let us remember all the babies born in inappropriate places, under inappropriate circumstances in the twenty-first century. God calls us to serve families in homeless shelters and displacement camps. People who are between countries and borders because of war or political status may seek the relative safety of a refugee camp. In 2012, the average population of a refugee camp was 11,400 people. Know that there are children in those camps. Depending on the host country, in order to discourage permanent settlement, sometimes schools are not even allowed. Camps are wretched places, with open latrines and tents, where children are at a high risk for disease, malnutrition, abuse, neglect, exploitation, and forced military recruitment, depending on the situation.

This Advent, let us remember that just as Joseph and Mary had to go to Bethlehem to obtain the appropriate documentation for residence in the Roman Empire, lack of documentation is problematic even in the twenty-first century. Homeless parents have no addresses. This makes it difficult to apply for jobs or to receive benefits that might help their situation. Immigration laws, poverty, and environmental disasters create orphans whose needs often fall through the safety net. By the power of the Holy Spirit, we are equipped "to care for orphans and widows in their distress" (James 1:27b). We have the power to make a difference in their lives. Let us work together, one by one, ten by ten, hundreds by hundreds and live out the message that was born in a baby, born in a manger, born in Bethlehem!

Discussion Questions
1. *What do you know about children who are displaced?*
2. *What are some of the causes for displaced families in your area?*

References
* Historical information on Fugitive Slave Acts: *www.history.com/topics/black-history/fugitive-slave-acts*

** *Twelve Years a Slave* (1853) is a memoir and slave narrative by Solomon Northup, as told to and edited by David Wilson. Northup, a black man who was born free in New York, details his kidnapping in Washington, D.C., and his subsequent sale into slavery. Available in film and book formats.

*** Julian Ursyn Niemcewicz, *Under Their Vine and Fig Tree: Travels Through America in 1797–1799, 1805 With Some Further Account of Life in New Jersey*, edited by Metchie J.E. Budka (Elizabeth, New Jersey: The Grassman Publishing Company, Inc., 1965); page 100.

LESSON FOUR
✳ Go, Tell It on the Mountain ✳

Go, tell it on the mountain,
over the hills and everywhere;
go, tell it on the mountain,
that Jesus Christ is born.

Verse 1
While shepherds kept their watching
o'er silent flocks by night,
behold throughout the heavens
there shone a holy light.

Verse 2
The shepherds feared and trembled
when lo! above the earth,
rang out the angel chorus
that hailed our Savior's birth.

Verse 3
Down in a lowly manger
the humble Christ was born,
and God sent us salvation
that blessed Christmas morn.

KEY VERSE: *The shepherds returned, glorifying and praising God for all they had heard and seen, as it had been told them.* (LUKE 2:20)

LUKE 2:8-20

8 Nearby shepherds were living in the fields, guarding their sheep at night. 9 The Lord's angel stood before them, the Lord's glory shone around them, and they were terrified. 10 The angel said, "Don't be afraid! Look! I bring good news to you—wonderful, joyous news for all people. 11 Your savior is born today in David's city. He is Christ the Lord. 12 This is a sign for you: you will find a newborn baby wrapped snugly and lying in a manger." 13 Suddenly a great assembly of the heavenly forces was with the angel praising God. They said, 14 "Glory to God in heaven, and on earth peace among those whom he favors." 15 When the angels returned to heaven,

the shepherds said to each other, "Let's go right now to Bethlehem and see what's happened. Let's confirm what the Lord has revealed to us." **16** They went quickly and found Mary and Joseph, and the baby lying in the manger. **17** When they saw this, they reported what they had been told about this child. **18** Everyone who heard it was amazed at what the shepherds told them. **19** Mary committed these things to memory and considered them carefully. **20** The shepherds returned home, glorifying and praising God for all they had heard and seen. Everything happened just as they had been told.

Meditation

Have you ever known someone who said they had received a message from God? Often, when a person says something like that (if he or she is not a preacher), we might look at them somewhat skeptically. One must only be aware of human history to realize that too often persons claiming to have messages from God are seeking justification for doing hurtful and violent things. So how do we keep ourselves open for God to tap us on the shoulder with a new revelation to share? How do we hear a message that just might change how people see one another, a message with the possibility of transforming the world? That message may not present itself in a blinding light as with Paul or in a choir of angels as with the shepherds. People might look at you strangely when you tell it. But you've got to tell a message from God . . . over the hills and everywhere you go!

Prayer
Dear God,
Give me the ears to hear, the insight to understand, the desire to share, the obedience to go. Instill in me the willingness to spread your message of salvation wherever I go so that others may see for themselves that you are real. In Jesus' name, amen.

Watching, Waiting, Wondering

The time comes when watching, waiting and wondering are inappropriate and ineffective. The shepherds had seen and heard enough. It was time for action; time to go to Bethlehem. Just as they made a decision to go there right away, the authority of the call to action resonated with people during the Civil Rights Movement. While "Go Tell It on the Mountain" is a spiritual that tells the story of what shepherds did after hearing the message of the angels, during the Movement, it was re-purposed as a call to action for freedom-loving people. No more watching, waiting or wondering.

Of course, by the middle of the twentieth century, black people had been wondering for a long time. When would they truly be free? When would "justice roll down like waters, and righteousness like an ever-flowing stream" (Amos 5:24)? When would they be recognized as human beings, wonderfully and marvelously created in the image of God (Psalm 139:14)? When would their contributions to American society be recognized, their rights as citizens upheld?

Black people had been watching and waiting for almost one hundred years. They had watched Reconstruction come and go, and waited as "Jim Crow" was established. They had watched people swing from trees in every state in the Union and waited for anti-lynching laws to pass in Congress (they never did). They had watched "sundown" signs go up in towns and waited as their fellow Americans legally covenanted them out of neighborhoods and redlined them out of property. They had watched while their sons proved themselves patriots in wars, only to be rewarded with race riots upon their return. They had waited (are waiting still) for fair housing, effective education systems, and productive economic opportunities. The time for wondering was over. They had seen and heard enough.

Discussion Questions

1. *What do you know about some of the issues mentioned: "Jim Crow," redlining, race riots before the 1950s, sundown laws?*
2. *Are there twenty-first century versions of these issues? If so, what are their effects on "post-racial" America?*

Go, Tell It on the Mountain: A New Song

One of the characteristics of the music of black, African-derived people is its functionality. Rather than adhering to rigid categories of music, a blues might be a spiritual, a spiritual might be a work song, and a gospel song may have been sung in the bar last night; it depends on the present situation and a word change or two. The music of Thomas Dorsey and Ray Charles are merely in a continuum of how black people have done music all along.

This is why so many of the freedom songs of the Civil Rights Movement are derived from spirituals. The Christmas spiritual "Go, Tell It on the Mountain" famously arranged by John Wesley Work, Jr., (1871–1925) is not the same one sung by Fannie Lou Hamer (1917–1977).* The melody is the same, the format is the same (starting with chorus rather than verse), and the call to action is the same; but Mrs. Hamer and the freedom singers changed the returning line "that Jesus Christ is born" to "to let my people go!"

Go, tell it on the mountain, over the hills and everywhere!
Go, tell it on the mountain to let my people go!

The verses no longer poignantly retell the story of shepherds, angels, and a baby but move to what can happen when you talk about a Savior who came to proclaim release to prisoners and liberate the oppressed (Luke 4:18).

1. Paul and Silas were bound in jail. Let my people go!
Had no money for to go their bail. Let my people go!

2. Paul and Silas began to shout. Let my people go!
Jail door opened and they walked out. Let my people go!

The tagline, "Let my people go!" is borrowed from the spiritual, "Go Down, Moses," reminding all that God's plan for physical freedom has always been part of God's relationship and plan for people. And the following verses mix elements from that traditional song with present realitites of pushing ahead for freedom.

3. You see those children dressed in red. Let my people go!
It must be the children that Moses led. Let my people go!

4. Who's that yonder dressed in black? Let my people go!
It must the hypocrites turning back! Let my people go!

The last verse demonstrates the sense of calling experienced by Fannie Lou Hamer and her trust in God. It communicates her understanding of the spiritual nature of the Civil Rights Movement and her belief in biblical righteousness.

5. Had a little book he gave to me. Let my people go!
Every page spelled victory. Let my people go!

Go, tell it on the mountain, over the hills and everywhere!
Go, tell it on the mountain to let my people go!

Discussion Questions
1. What other spirituals were used as a basis for freedom songs?
2. How can we adjust other kinds of church songs into rallying cries for justice?

Messengers (Luke 2:8-20)

As they watched their flocks in the hills of Judea, the shepherds witnessed a terrifying sight, as first one angel and then a multitude appeared! An angel represented the very presence of God, the word of God. They believed that anyone who saw God would surely die (Exodus 33:20). As translated from biblical languages, *malak*, (Hebrew as in Malachi, "my messenger") and *angelos* (Greek as in *evangel*, "good news") both words mean messenger. Angels were emissaries between heaven and earth, carrying messages from God. Of course, the shepherds were afraid.

Sometimes we use the word angel to refer to a human messenger with special service to God. The most important matter regarding angels, whether human or divine, is in discerning their message. The presence of an angel requires that we be open and ready to receive. We have all been in the presence of an angel at some point in life.

Famous for saying that she was "sick and tired of being sick and tired," Fannie Lou Hamer was an angel of the Civil Rights Movement. After hearing a sermon delivered by Rev. James Bevel, an organizer of SNCC (Student Nonviolent Coordinating Committee), she took up his challenge to become a registered voter. After her attempt to register, her family was evicted from the plantation where they lived and worked. Rather than being afraid, this freed her to work as an activist because she determined that "they" could do to her only what they had been trying to do her whole life—kill her. At a rally in Indianola, Mississippi, Hamer raised her voice to inspire communal singing and encourage confidence. After this, she was sought out to lead singing at rallies across the South. To civil rights leaders and workers, she was "the lady who sings hymns." To President Lyndon Johnson, she was "that illiterate woman."

While Hamer received the minimal education the state of Mississippi designed for its black citizens, she was neither inarticulate nor dumb. In 1964, as one of the founders and organizers of the Freedom Mississippi Democratic Party, she eloquently brought a message to the Democratic National Convention that a segregated official Mississippi delegation was undemocratic. She told of the problems Blacks had in trying to register and of her own brutal beating by police in 1963. She told Senator Hubert Humphrey, who hoped to gain the Democratic Party's nomination for Vice President that his position was not more important than the lives of 400,000 black people and that she "going to pray to Jesus for him." The attention garnered by her advocacy forced the party to change its rules so that by 1968, Fannie Lou Hamer was indeed one of the delegates from Mississippi to the national convention. She was a messenger for God, sharing news of God's desire for justice for all people.

The shepherds received a message of good news and became messengers themselves. The angels had given them the birth announcement of The Messiah. They had given the shepherds instructions on what to do—"Go to Bethlehem and see!" And they had glorified God, promising peace on those whom God favored. After a brief discussion, the shepherds followed the instructions. They found Jesus and his family just as the angels had promised and on the return journey, they told people about him. People were amazed at their story, none more than Mary, who would cherish this memory. And then the celebration continued. Like the angelic messengers, the shepherds praised and glorified God for all they had experienced.

Discussion Questions
1. *Who are some of the angels in your community?*
2. *What power do governments have to affect the well being of people?*

Twenty-first Century Nativity: Telling the Story

The world is always in need of a message from God. This is as true during the Advent season as it is in any season. The angels, the shepherds, the slaves, and Fannie Lou Hamer all had a sense of urgency about spreading the good news of Jesus' birth, the good news of peace on earth, the good news of a Savior, and the good news of God's justice! The good news of Jesus Christ gave those captured in America's slave system hope, enabling them to transcend their grim reality with knowledge that God truly reigns "over the hills and everywhere!" Through study, prayer, and fellowship with the people of God, we cooperate with the Holy Spirit in equipping ourselves to be messengers in a world that needs to hear more about God's love and justice.

Upon receiving the news that life did not have to remain as it was, that inclusion in a more just America was possible, there were those like Fanny Lou Hamer, who like the shepherds used their voices to spread the word. They went and told everyone they could find, glorifying God in the process. Fanny Lou Hamer went from the church house to the villages and hamlets throughout the South, all the way to the national arena of the National Democratic Convention, which became a global stage. She put her body on the line knowing that all they could do was kill her.

The imperative in "Go Tell It on the Mountain" reminds us to tell the story about a child, who faced homelessness, poverty, lack of documentation, injustice, death and possible imprisonment. By focusing on the gift of the Christ Child and the light of God in the lives of every child, we can be agents to revolutionize our world, one child at a time, to begin a process of healing. The gift of a child is more precious than wealth, status, or recognition. We radiate the light of Christ when we show love and compassion for all children everywhere.

We should never neglect to tell the story of how God delivered a people from slavery, whether Hebrew or African American. We should never neglect to tell how God is able to rescue each one from the slavery of sin and death.

In telling the story, we like the angels and the shepherds, glorify God. When we tell the story, in a spirit of gratitude, and refuse to let life's circumstances dictate our own expectations about justice, loving self, God and neighbor, we possess the hope that Jesus' birth means that all things can be made new!

This Advent season, let us remember that we are messengers of hope. By the power of the Holy Spirit, we can be obedient to the mandate given all disciples of Jesus Christ: to bring good news to the poor, help the blind and those in need of healing, to advocate for the oppressed, and relieve the suffering. Jesus Christ is born! Now is the time! God has favored us this year and every year to live in the newness of life by working towards the realization of God's kingdom and telling the good news. Go! Tell it from the storefront churches, from imposing church edifices, from homeless shelters, in the displacement camps, on street corners, in apartment complexes, in gated communities, in the prisons, in the sandboxes—everywhere!

Discussion Questions

1. *Do you demonstrate a sense of urgency concerning the Second Coming of Christ?*
2. *What are some ways to share the good news of Jesus Christ during this Advent season?*

References

* Fannie Lou Hamer's version of "Go, Tell It on the Mountain" on YouTube: *http://youtu.be/kxRfT12Sojw*

The Veterans of Hope Project at the Iliff School of Theology, Denver, Colorado: *http://www.veteransofhope.org*

❋ LEADER GUIDE ❋

To the Leader

The Leader Guide will help you prepare to lead the lessons as well as organize class time. It is included in this resource as an economical device to help those who are facilitating this study for adult learners. It has been updated from the 2003 edition. Before getting into the lessons, be sure to read the Opening Meditation and the Introduction on pages 4 and 5. These will set the stage by illuminating the nature of Advent and of the African American spiritual. Encourage the participants to read them as well.

THE MUSIC

Because each lesson is based on an African American spiritual, the music is crucial in teaching the lessons. While the lyrics are provided at the beginning of each of the lessons, you will need to download the digital song files, using this link: *AbingdonPress.com/MaryHadABaby*. The lyrics correspond to this particular arrangement. However, rather than listening to each song, you may also choose to have the participants sing each song as part of a devotional time that would include:

1. Listening to or singing the music.
2. Reading the Scripture, the Key Verse, and the story passage.
3. Reading the meditation.
4. Praying.

THE BIBLE LESSON

Prepare each lesson ahead of time. Read through the lessons, along with all of the referenced Scripture. This study is particular to the Advent season, with an emphasis of preparing our hearts for the Second Coming of Jesus Christ. During Advent, we also prepare to celebrate the birth of Jesus as a baby. Allow the lessons to help you meditate on the reason for the season in ways that will communicate joy and expectation for the participants. Each lesson begins with an introduction entitled "Watching, Waiting, Wondering" in order to facilitate the expectations of Advent.

Each lesson will end with a section entitled "Twenty-first Century Nativity." It will help summarize and contextualize biblical and cultural/historical teaching in a way that keeps the community grounded in Advent, what we need to do as we continue to look for Jesus to come back. Each lesson will help the participants take stock of how the past affects the present and the future and what the Christ Child might expect from disciples on behalf of all of God's children.

Many of the sections have discussion questions at the end. Utilize them in the best way to stimulate learning for the participants. Additionally, the Leader Guide includes ice-breakers, additional questions, activities, and information that you may find helpful. As you plan your class time, make decisions about what to include. Or you may find that you need the additional information to fill in the time and enhance conversation.

THE GROUP MEETING

Be sure to bring everything that you may need to create a stimulating learning and worship environment. You may need a computer to play the downloadable songs or some hymnals if you are choosing to have the group sing. Bring visuals that will help the participants stay focused. A miniature nativity scene would be perfect. Traditionally, the baby Jesus is not added to the nativity scene until Christmas Day; so using this kind of visual will remind the participants that we are waiting for Jesus to come.

Pray throughout the preparation process. Ask God to work with you as you apply your mind and heart to study. God will increase your ability to be fruitful and effective with your adult participants if you are willing to put in the necessary time. Take notes as you study. Be ready for new insights. Do additional research to resolve any questions in your mind.

During class, facilitate the conversation so that all participants have an opportunity to contribute. By listening patiently to each expression, you encourage all participants to do the same. At the same time, be mindful of persons who may monopolize the conversation or offer judgmental opinions. Be as gracious as possible in steering the discussion back to the material at hand. Encourage the participants to read the lesson before the class meets so that they too can bring insights and new information. Don't be afraid to move away from the text, even as you want to cover the material included during the designated time. Remember that the ultimate goal is that you and your students experience the fellowship of growing together in Jesus Christ.

LESSON ONE: Mary Had a Baby, page 7

LUKE 1:30-31; MATTHEW 1:18-25

KEY VERSE: *Look! You will conceive and give birth to a son, and you will name him Jesus.* (LUKE 1:31)

YOUR PREPARATION

✳ Review the song lyrics as you listen to "Mary Had a Baby."
✳ Read the Scripture lesson.
✳ Before reading the Meditation, read "Mary's Song" (Luke 1:46-55). You may choose to refer to it during class.
✳ Review the directions for the ice-breaker and decide whether to include it.
✳ Take time to research and review the additional information included. You may choose to read through the genealogies of Jesus in Matthew 1:1-17 and Luke 3:23-38.
✳ Remember to pray.

DURING CLASS

Opening (with an ice-breaker)
To engage participants immediately, play the name game as they arrive.
   A. The first person, which could be you, gives his or her name, placing an adjective or description in front of the name.
   B. The second person repeats what the first person said and then adds his or her own name and descriptor, and so on. Examples: "I am Musical Marilyn." Second person: "You are Musical Marilyn, and I am Dynamite David." Third person: "Dynamite David and Musical Marilyn, I'm Victorious Ms. Vee!"
   C. Since participants will continue to arrive during the game, ask those who have had a turn to repeat their names for the newcomers. Allow 2–3 minutes.
✳ Have the participants open their books to page 7 and direct their attention to the lyrics. Play the music for "Mary Had a Baby" as the participants read the words.
✳ Have the class read the Key Verse in unison.
✳ Ask a volunteer to read the Scripture lesson aloud.
✳ Read the Meditation on page 8 aloud.
✳ Have the class read in unison the Prayer.

Watching, Waiting, Wondering (Luke 1:30-31), page 8
✳ Ask a volunteer to read this section.
✳ Refer the participants to page 38 to see the Hebrew names for God; or simply mention that there are many names, listing a few examples.
✳ Engage the participants with the Discussion Questions concerning family naming traditions and name acceptance in society. You may choose to include this commentary: Sometimes celebrities give their

children unusual names: Blue Ivy (Beyonce and Jay Z), for example. In the African American community, some have moved toward combination names (parts of father and mother's names) or made-up names and have moved away from the biblical, ancestral, and African names. What do you think of these practices?

Names for God and the Meanings
El Shaddai (Lord God Almighty)
El Elyon (The Most High God)
Adonai (Lord, Master)
Yahweh-YHWH (the Hebrew name for God, often pronounced *Jehovah*)
Jehovah Nissi (The Lord My Banner)
Jehovah-Raah (The Lord My Shepherd)
Jehovah Rapha (The Lord That Heals)
Jehovah Shammah (The Lord Is There)
Jehovah Tsidkenu (The Lord Our Righteousness)
Jehovah Mekoddishkem (The Lord Who Sanctifies You)
El Olam (The Everlasting God)
Elohim (God)
Qanna (Jealous)
Jehovah Jireh (The Lord Will Provide)
Jehovah Shalom (The Lord Is Peace)
Jehovah Sabaoth (The Lord of Hosts)

This Train Is Bound for Glory, page 9
✳ Have several participants take turns reading this section aloud, one paragraph at a time.
✳ Engage the participants with the discussion questions by reminding them that the creation of spirituals and of a Christian identity occurred over time. Africans did not walk the plank from the slave ship, singing spirituals.
✳ You may also choose to give this commentary: Many slaves lived in "Advent mode"—expecting/anticipating. What does it mean to live in perpetual expectation? After long periods of time, how does one keep hope alive? Do unfulfilled hopes strengthen or weaken faith?

Immanuel (Matthew 1:18-25), page 10
✳ Participants may find it interesting to compare the genealogy of Jesus found in Matthew 1:1-17 with the one in Luke 3:23-38. Do not let the discussion take more time than necessary. Point out that the genealogies were included as proofs so that people of Jewish descent would believe.
✳ Ask participants take turns reading this section aloud, a paragraph at a time.

✳ Be prepared to read aloud Deuteronomy 22:13-21, concerning the stoning of pregnant unmarried women. Have participants comment on Joseph's involvement in protecting his wife and providing for her child. How is his behavior an example in the twenty-first century?

More Discussion Questions

a. How can churches and communities promote the understanding that "each child carries the light of God within"?

b. Do African Americans still look for a potential liberator?

Twenty-first Century Nativity: Honoring Mother and Child, page 12

✳ After the first two paragraphs are read aloud, take a moment for participants to discuss the question at the end of paragraph 2: "What would happen if we were to greet every birth as an indication of the promise of God's love and saving purpose in the world?"

✳ Continue the reading, and end the lesson with a brief discussion.

✳ Remind the participants to read the next lesson before the next meeting.

✳ Ask for a participant to close out in prayer.

LESSON TWO: Rise Up, Shepherd, and Follow, page 14

LUKE 2:15; MATTHEW 2:1-12

KEY VERSE: *When they heard the king, they went; and look, the star they had seen in the east went ahead of them until it stood over the place where the child was.* (MATTHEW 2:9)

YOUR PREPARATION

✳ Review the song lyrics as you listen to "Rise Up, Shepherd, and Follow." The words for the third verse begin at the bottom of page 17.

✳ Read the Scripture lesson.

✳ In reading the Meditation, locate and read all of the Scripture references.

✳ Look for either a photo or computer image of the constellation "The Big Dipper." Be able to identify the North Star.

✳ Take time to research and review the additional information included.

✳ Many adults like arts and crafts. If you choose to, plan to have the participants decorate a small gourd. Have on hand a cleaned gourd for each participant, some paint pens, and paper towels and other items for cleaning up. Have the supplies available at the beginning of class.

✳ Remember to pray.

DURING CLASS

Opening
- ✳ Have either a photo or a ready image on your computer of the constellation "The Big Dipper." As participants arrive, let them see it.
- ✳ If you have chosen for participants to do the craft, have supplies ready.
- ✳ Have the participants open their books to page 14. Direct their attention to the lyrics. Play the music for "Rise Up, Shepherd, and Follow" as the participants read the words.
- ✳ Have the class read the Key Verse in unison.
- ✳ Ask a volunteer to read the Scripture lesson.
- ✳ Read the Meditation on page 15 aloud.
- ✳ Have the class read the Prayer in unison.

Watching, Waiting, Wondering (Luke 2:15), page 15
- ✳ Get a volunteer to read this section.
- ✳ Engage participants in the Discussion Questions.

Arise, Shine, for Your Light Has Come, page 16
- ✳ Have the class take turns reading this section, one person for each paragraph.
- ✳ Discussion Questions: While most are familiar with the names Gabriel Prosser (1800), Denmark Vesey (1822), and Nat Turner (1831), who planned rebellions, too often black people have been accused of being passive and accepting of enslavement. You may choose to have the participants turn to this page to see this short list (from over 300) of slave rebellions in the U.S.

1663: In Gloucester County, Virginia, a conspiracy between black slave and white indentured servants was betrayed.

1711: Led by Sebastian, a group of Maroons (runaway slaves) terrorized colonists in South Carolina. There were about 50 communities of Maroons living in the woods and mountains of the Carolinas and Virginia.

1712: In New York City, twelve slaves were executed for their participation in a rebellion. Six others committed suicide.

1723: Based on rumor and evidence, precautions were taken to foil a plan by Negroes to burn the city of Boston.

1739: In a series of rebellions starting on September 9, armed black slaves marched from Charleston, South Carolina to the Stono River to St. John's Parish toward freedom in Spanish Florida. At least 50 Whites and even more Blacks died.

1741: The oppression of 1,700 Blacks led to the New York City Conspiracy in which black secret societies planned a series of fires from New Jersey to

Long Island, which upon investigation, revealed a plot to kill white men, seize white women, and burn down the city. Seventy Blacks were exiled to places like Newfoundland and Saint-Domingue (Haiti). Thirty were executed.

1811: On January 8, led by mulatto slave driver Charles Delondes, on the Andry sugar plantation in the German Coast area near New Orleans, 25 slaves rose up in rebellion. Their numbers grew as they moved from the well-supplied plantation to others. Upon running out of ammunition, they surrendered to U.S. troops, led by Wade Hampton of South Carolina. About 100 Blacks were executed, while another 20 had died in battle.

1816: Three hundred Blacks and 20 Native Americans held Fort Blount on Apalachicola Bay in Florida for several days before being overcome by U.S. troops.

Searching and Seeking (Matthew 2:1-12), page 17

If you have chosen for the participants to create a gourd decoration, direct them to get a gourd. They will need to share the paint pens. Instruct them to quietly decorate their gourds with holiday greetings, Scripture, or just color while the lesson continues.

✳ Read this section as the participants decorate their gourds.

✳ They may continue to work as they discuss the question.

✳ You may also choose to play this selection "We Are," by Sweet Honey in the Rock, on a computer: *https://www.youtube.com/watch?v=CsEic8ORhqc*. The refrain is: "For each child that's born, a morning star rises and sings to the universe who we are."

Twenty-first Century Nativity: Following the Light, page 19

✳ Ask someone to read the first paragraph aloud.

✳ In reading the second paragraph, identify someone to also read the referenced passages: Matthew 2:12-15 and 2:16.

✳ Depending on the time, you may choose to have the participants turn to this page to see these statistics or you may simply refer to them.*

✳ Have a brief discussion.

✳ Remind the participants to read Lesson Three before the next meeting.

✳ Ask for a participant to close out in prayer.

* According to research by the Children's Defense Fund in Spring 2014:

• Each day 7 children and teens die from gun violence.

• A majority (66 percent) of eighth graders in public school are unable to read or compute (do math) at grade level.

• Each day 4,028 children (one every 21 seconds) are arrested.

• Each day 1,825 children are confirmed to have been abused.

• The average household wealth in black homes is $6,314; the average in white homes is $110,500.

LESSON THREE: Children, Go Where I Send Thee

LUKE 2:1-7

KEY VERSE: *Since Joseph belonged to David's house and family line, he went up from the city of Nazareth in Galilee to David's city, called Bethlehem, in Judea.* (LUKE 2:4)

YOUR PREPARATION

* ✳ Review the song lyrics as you listen to "Children, Go Where I Send Thee."
* ✳ Read the Scripture lesson.
* ✳ Read the Meditation.*
* ✳ Take time to research and review the additional information included. Be aware of the Solomon Northrup (also Northup) story and the folk literature mentioned. You may choose to go to the local library, check out a copy of *The People Could Fly: American Black Folktales*, by Virginia Hamilton, and bring it to class.
* ✳ Remember to pray.

* Note

The movement of African Americans from the South to points North, East, and West, and from rural areas to more urbanized areas even in the South from 1900 to 1960 is called The Great Migration. The book *The Warmth of Other Suns: the Epic Story of America's Great Migration* (2010), by Pulitzer prize-winning journalist Isabel Wilkerson, details the story of several families who went through this process. Artist Jacob Lawrence's series of murals depicting the struggles of this event, *Migration of the Negro* (now called *The Migration Series*), was featured at the Museum of Modern Art in 1941.

DURING CLASS

Opening

* ✳ Have the participants open their books to page 21, and direct their attention to the lyrics. Play the music for "Children, Go Where I Send Thee" as the participants read the words.
* ✳ Have the class read the Key Verse in unison.
* ✳ Ask a volunteer to read the Scripture lesson aloud.
* ✳ Read the Meditation on page 22 aloud.

✳ Have the class read the Prayer in unison.
✳ Have a brief discussion about The Great Migration. Most black families have experienced this one way or the other, being the part of the family that moved or being the part of the family that stayed in the South.

Watching, Waiting, Wondering. page 22
✳ Ask volunteers to read this section read aloud.
✳ If some participants saw the movie *12 Years a Slave*, briefly discuss it.
✳ You may choose to share some of the following information about "slave catching" in 1851* or have the participants to turn to this page.
✳ Depending on the time, engage the class in the discussion questions.

* In 1851:
• A Mr. Miller was killed in Maryland as he was returning to Nottingham, Pennsylvania, with a free black girl who had been kidnapped from his house and taken to Baltimore.
• A slave catcher named Gorsuch was killed by free Blacks in Christiana, Pennsylvania, when he refused to leave the house of William Parker, a free Black.
• In Boston, black abolitionists rescued Shadrach Minkins from a courtroom to prevent his return to slavery.

A Theology of Movement, page 23
✳ If you have the book *The People Could Fly*, pass it around. The cover illustration is by Leo and Diane Dillon.
✳ Encourage the participants to briefly sing one the songs mentioned in this section.
✳ Discuss the commandment given by Jesus in terms of global evangelism.

African Americans are often criticized for not participating in global missions. There are historical and financial reasons for this. Often black people do not have the kinds of jobs with leave that will allow them to do such trips, which are fairly expensive. Additionally, from a historical perspective, African Americans were discouraged from evangelizing in colonial Africa. A good example of this is Mary McLeod Bethune, whose original intent upon attending the Moody Bible Institute in Chicago (1894) was to become a missionary in Africa. She was told that black missionaries were not needed.

Nevertheless, we have the example of former slave Lott Carey (1780–1828), who bought his own freedom 1813 and was the first African American and Baptist missionary to Africa. In 1821, he led a missionary team with a focus on evangelism, health, and education and established the Providence Baptist Church in Monrovia, Liberia. The Lott Carey Foreign Mission Convention continues to exist and partners with indigenous communities throughout Africa. Another early example of a black missionary is Betsey Stockton, who from 1822–1823 was part of a Presbyterian mission team to the Sandwich Islands (Hawaii). In addition to caring for the young white children in her charge, she maintained a school for the Hawaiians on Maui, teaching English and the gospel.

So, Where Would They Go? (Luke 2:1-7), page 25

＊ Have participants consult biblical maps as this section is read. Point out Rome, Syria, Palestine, Nazareth, Galilee, Bethlehem, and Jerusalem.
＊ Ask: What does it mean to be "undocumented"? Is this something about which Christians should be concerned?
＊ Ask: Are tax laws something about which Christians should be concerned?

Twenty-first Century Nativity: Going Where the Children Are, page 26

＊ After reading this section, engage in a brief discussion, using the questions provided.
＊ Remind the participants to read the next lesson before the next meeting.
＊ Ask for a participant to close out in prayer.

LESSON FOUR: Go, Tell It on the Mountain, page 28

LUKE 2:8-20

KEY VERSE: *The shepherds returned, glorifying and praising God for all they had heard and seen, as it had been told them.* (LUKE 2:20)

YOUR PREPARATION

＊ Review the song lyrics as you listen to "Go, Tell It on the Mountain."
＊ Read the Scripture lesson and the Meditation.
＊ Read the entire lesson, along with all Scripture references.
＊ Listen to Fannie Lou Hamer's version of "Go, Tell It on the Mountain."
＊ Review these terms: *Jim Crow, redlining, sundown laws, restrictive covenants, lynching.*
＊ Remember to pray.

Sundown laws: A method by which to keep a town, city, or neighborhood purposely all white. Often signs were posted at the borders, warning N---- to not let the sun go down on their presence in town. This happened also with Chinese and Native Americans, depending on the locality.

Redlining: The practice of grading neighborhoods, making it easier or more difficult to obtain FHA loans

Restrictive covenants: Agreements with real estate agents to not sell to people of color

Jim Crow: Laws and practices (1877–1965) that instituted racial segregation

Lynching: Murder by mob through hanging, burning, or shooting, inclusive of maiming and torturing

DURING CLASS

Opening
* ✳ Have the participants open their books to page 28, and direct their attention to the lyrics. Play the music for "Go, Tell It on the Mountain" as the participants read the words.
* ✳ Have the class read the Key Verse in unison.
* ✳ Ask a volunteer to read the Scripture lesson aloud.
* ✳ Read the Meditation on page 29 aloud.
* ✳ Have the class read the Prayer in unison.
* ✳ Have a brief discussion about whether participants have ever heard someone say that he or she had received a message from God. Ask: What was your reaction?

Watching, Waiting, Wondering, page 29
* ✳ Have this section read in its entirety.
* ✳ Engage the discussion questions.
* ✳ Depending on your time, you may choose to have the participants turn to pages 45–46 or share the following information with them as you deem needed.

* Notes
1. "Race" riots are part of the American landscape. At first, they were anti-Catholic and immigrant "race" riots. From the Colonial Era through the mid-1800s, Protestant nativists rioted against newly arriving Irish Catholics and Germans on the East Coast. In the 1850s, in response to the Gold Rush in California, the groups that were rioted against expanded to Mexican, Chilean, and Chinese immigrants. In the South, during the late 1800s and early 1900s, Italians were subjected to racial violence, with one of the largest mass lynchings occurring in New Orleans (1891), wherein eleven Italians were murdered.

Over the past 120 years or so, most racial violence has been directed against black people:

1887 in Louisiana: Sugar plantation workers (mostly black) demonstrated for higher wages. They were met by state-sponsored violence that supported the mob-killing of at least 20 and as many as 300 Blacks.

1891 in Omaha, Nebraska: Joe Coe was removed from his jail cell and lynched by a mob of 10,000 ethnic immigrants after he was suspected of attacking a white woman.

1906 in Atlanta: Black people sought asylum at Gammon School of Theology and Clark University.

1906 in Springfield, Ohio: There were riots against black people.

1908 in Springfield, Illinois: Riots described as "The Race War in the North" required 4,200 militia to quell. Most of the black populace of that city fled or was forced to leave after a black man who had been married to a white woman for 30 years was lynched. This riot helped to inspire the founding of the National Association for the Advancement of Colored People (NAACP) by 1909.

1919 (April–October): "Red Summer" -- 76 black people were killed in post-WWI in 25 race riots across the nation. One of the first riots was incited by a white man enraged by the sight of a black man in a military uniform.

2. In 1917, Leonidas C. Dyer, a Republican from St. Louis, Missouri, in reaction to race riots against black people in his district over employment issues and failure to prosecute perpetrators of lynching, introduced a bill to make lynching a federal felony, with reparations paid to the victims' families. From 1922–1924, despite support from President Warren G. Harding, the bill failed to pass a Senate controlled by filibustering Southern Democrats. In 2005, the Senate sponsored a resolution apologizing for its failure to enact this bill and others from 1890–1952, when they were most needed.

Go, Tell It on the Mountain: A New Song, page 30
* After reading the first paragraph, if you have the equipment, share Fannie Lou Hamer's version of this song. See page 34.
* Continue reading this section. Repeat the song as desired.
* Do the discussion questions on page 31.
* Find a simple church song that is popular with your congregation, and invite participants to alter the words to create a song that advocates for justice.

Messengers (Luke 2:8-20), page 31
* Invite four participants to read one paragraph each aloud.
* Discuss the meaning of *angel.*

✳ Invite the participants to turn to page 47 to read more about the Mississippi Freedom Democratic Party*, or share some information as you have time.

✳ Engage the participants in the discussion questions.

* The Mississippi Freedom Democratic Party was created in 1964 by African Americans from Mississippi, with the assistance of the Student Nonviolent Coordinating Committee (SNCC) and the Council of Federated Organizations (COFO) to challenge the legitimacy of the Whites-only Mississippi delegation. It was an outcome of black people attempting to register to vote and to actually vote but being denied. In June of 1963, they organized a Freedom Ballot in which close to 80,000 people cast ballots for an integrated slate of candidates.

Twenty-first Century Nativity: Telling the Story, page 33

✳ Divide the group into two small groups.

✳ As they read this last section, each group is to design an Advent project that is to be carried out with the expectation of the Second Coming of Jesus Christ. Ask: Keeping in mind all of the issues we have discussed during this Advent study, what do you want to be found doing when Christ returns? While we celebrate Advent during a designated time, Advent is truly all of the time, for we do not know the day or the hour of his return.

✳ Have the small groups come back together in the large group and tell what they have started planning.

✳ End the class with everyone praying The Lord's Prayer. Emphasize "Your kingdom come, your will be done on earth as it is in heaven."

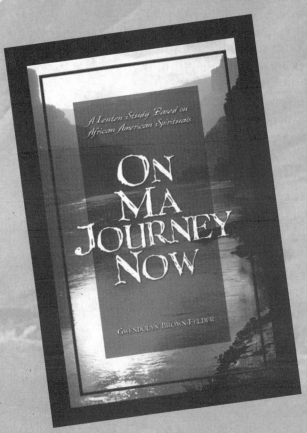